```
          Merwin, E. author.
j         A haunted Titanic
910.9163  CHJNFG
Mer       34711203647914
```

D1786289

Charlestown-Clark Co Public Library
51 Clark Road
Charlestown, IN 47111-1972

A Haunted Titanic

by E. Merwin

Consultant: Melinda E. Ratchford, EdD
Titanic Historian and Associate Professor
Sister Christine Beck Department of Education
Belmont Abbey College
Belmont, North Carolina

BEARPORT
PUBLISHING

New York, New York

Credits

Cover top, *Titanic* Painting © Ken Marschall; Cover bottom, © iStockphoto.com/ilbusca; 4, © ClassicStock/Alamy; 5, *Titanic* Painting © Ken Marschall; 6TL, © Chronicle/Alamy; 6TR, © Paul Fearn/Alamy; 6B, Wikimedia/tinyurl.com/y8n628q6/public domain; 7T, Wikimedia/tinyurl.com/y7d2ceo7/public domain; 7B, Wikimedia/tinyurl.com/y7gu2bsh/public domain; 8T, © Everett Historical/Shutterstock.com; 8BL, © Peter Muhly/Alamy; 8BR, © Chronicle/Alamy; 9, Wikimedia/tinyurl.com/yamg7ufb/public domain; 10L, © Chronicle/Alamy; 10R, © Chronicle/Alamy; 11L, Elliot Brown/tinyurl.com/yccj4dd6/CC BY 2.0; 11R, © John Keates/Alamy; 12, Wikimedia/tinyurl.com/y844tp63/public domain; 13, Image courtesy of Lori Johnston, RMS Titanic Expedition 2003, NOAA-OE; 14L, © Mary Evans/The National Archives, London, England/age footstock; 14R, © The National Archives/MT 9/920/C; 15, W.Rebel/tinyurl.com/ycysb3fp/CC-BY 2.0; 16T, Wikimedia/tinyurl.com/ycrpqcgp/public domain; 16B, © Chronicle/Alamy; 17, William J. Parker/tinyurl.com/y8cfp2ju/public domain; 18, © Lee Brown/Alamy; 18T, © Manor Photography/Alamy; 18B, © Manor Photography/Alamy; 20, © Mary Evans Picture Library Ltd/age footstock; 21T, © Paul Fearn/Alamy; 21B, Zeete/tinyurl.com/y8mu3529/CC-BY-SA 4.0; 22T, © Chronicle/Alamy; 22B, © Everett Historical/Shutterstock.com; 23, © Everett Collection/Shutterstock.com; 24TL, © Photo by Michel Boutefeu/Getty Images; 24TR, © EML/Shutterstock.com; 24C, © Photo by Matt Cardy/Getty Images; 24B, © Photo by Michel Boutefeu/Getty Images; 25L, © Photo by David Paul Morris/Getty Images; 25R, © marlenka/iStock/Getty Images Plus; 26L, © Mikhail hoboton Popo/Shutterstock.com; 26R, © george logan/Alamy; 27T, © Everett Historical/Shutterstock.com; 27B, © Stephen Barnes/Alamy; 28–29, Wikimedia/tinyurl.com/y8n628q6/public domain; 28L, © Anneka/Shutterstock.com; 29T, *The Sinking of the Titanic* (gouache on paper), Jackson, Peter (1922–2003)/Private Collection/© Look and Learn/Bridgeman Images; 29B, © AGCuesta/Shutterstock.com; 31, © WENN US/Alamy; 32, The New York Times/tinyurl.com/ydauec2u/public domain.

Publisher: Kenn Goin
Senior Editor: Joyce Tavolacci
Creative Director: Spencer Brinker
Photo Research: Editorial Directions, Inc.

Library of Congress Cataloging-in-Publication Data

Names: Merwin, E., author. Title: A haunted Titanic / by E. Merwin ; consultant: Melinda E. Ratchford, EdD, Associate Professor, Sister Christine Beck, Department of Education, Belmont Abbey College, Belmont, North Carolina.
Description: New York, New York : Bearport Publishing Company, Inc., [2018] |
Series: Titanica | Includes webography. | Includes bibliographical references and index. | Audience: Ages: 5-8.
Identifiers: LCCN 2017034363 (print) | LCCN 2017049942 (ebook) |
ISBN 9781684024919 (ebook) | ISBN 9781684024339 (Library) Subjects: LCSH: Titanic (Steamship)—Juvenile literature. | Shipwrecks—North Atlantic Ocean—Juvenile literature. | Haunted places—Juvenile literature.
Classification: LCC G530.T6 (ebook) | LCC G530.T6 M8 2018 (print) | DDC 910.9163/4—dc23
LC record available at https://lccn.loc.gov/2017034363

Copyright © 2018 Bearport Publishing Company, Inc. All rights reserved. No part of this publication may be reproduced in whole or in part, stored in a retrieval system, or transmitted in any form or by any means, electronic, mechanical, photocopying, recording, or otherwise, without written permission from the publisher.

For more information, write to Bearport Publishing Company, Inc., 45 West 21st Street, Suite 3B, New York, New York 10011. Printed in the United States of America.

10 9 8 7 6 5 4 3 2 1

CONTENTS

Death Dream 4
Book of Doom 6
Ghostly Goodbyes 8
No Place Like Home 10
Underwater Tomb 12
Phantom Messages 14
Halifax Hauntings 16
Dining with the Dead 18
Eternal Vacation 20
Afterlife Reporter 22
Dead on Display 24
Rest in Peace 26

Titanic: Visions of Doom 28
Glossary 30
Bibliography 31
Read More 31
Learn More Online 31
Index 32
About the Author 32

DEATH DREAM

It was the night of April 14, 1912. Alone and dying at a shelter in Kirkcudbright, Scotland, Jessie Sayre, a young **orphan**, tossed and turned in a **feverish** sleep. Captain W. Rex Sowden, the director of the shelter, was called to comfort her. Meanwhile, hundreds of miles away, a huge ship called the *Titanic* cruised in the dark waters of the Atlantic Ocean toward an unseen iceberg.

Yet somehow Jessie sensed the *Titanic*'s **doom**. "Hold my hand, Captain," she cried. "I am so afraid. Can't you see that big ship sinking in the water?" Sowden told her it was only a dream, but Jessie insisted. "Look at all those people who are drowning. Someone called Wally is playing a fiddle and coming toward you." Then Jessie fell into a **coma** and died at 11:40 PM— the same time an iceberg struck the *Titanic*'s **hull**.

The *Titanic*, a British passenger ship, was the largest boat in the world when it was built in 1911. It was thought to be unsinkable.

BOOK OF DOOM

Jessie Sayre was not the first person to imagine the doomed ship and its passengers. Fourteen years earlier in 1898, Morgan Robertson had written a book about an **ocean liner** that was a **dead ringer** for the *Titanic*. Both ships were around 800 feet (244 m) long and could cruise at high speeds. Even spookier, Robertson named his ship the *Titan*.

The *Titanic*

Morgan Robertson's book was called *Futility, or The Wreck of the Titan*.

Just like the *Titanic,* the ship in Robertson's story was sailing across the North Atlantic in April when it struck an iceberg. How did this writer **foresee** the terrible accident long before the *Titanic* was ever built? No one will ever know.

An iceberg thought to be the one that struck the *Titanic*

Robertson's ship, similar to the *Titanic,* did not have enough lifeboats for all its passengers.

A lifeboat from the *Titanic*

GHOSTLY GOODBYES

After the real *Titanic* struck the iceberg on April 14, 1912, millions of gallons of seawater gushed into the ship. At 2:20 AM, the ship cracked in two and sank. As in Jessie Sayre's **premonition**, more than 1,500 people drowned in the freezing water. Captain W. Rex Sowden was shocked to discover later that his friend, Wally Hartley, was among them. Wally, who was *Titanic*'s bandmaster, had played his violin to help calm passengers up until the ship sank.

The *Titanic* sank in less than three hours.

Violinist and *Titanic*'s bandleader, Wallace "Wally" Hartley

Wally wasn't the only victim to speak from beyond the grave that terrible night. In Southampton, England—home to more than 500 *Titanic* crewmen who had died—wives told of terrible nightmares. Many heard their names called out in the dark. The next day, they learned what had happened to the ship. Many women believed their loved ones had appeared to say a ghostly goodbye.

A boy sells newspapers the day after the *Titanic* sank.

The *Titanic* had about 900 crew members. Of the 685 workers from the city of Southampton, 538 died during the disaster.

No Place Like Home

That same night, Eleanor, the wife of *Titanic*'s captain, Edward John Smith, also reported a ghostly visit. She was in her bedroom when suddenly the door flung open. A misty figure resembling her husband appeared. He then walked to a window and **vanished**. That was not, however, the last time Captain Smith's spirit was seen.

Eleanor Smith

Captain Edward John Smith

Nearly one hundred years later, a British couple, Neil and Louise Bonner, bought Captain Smith's boyhood home to rent it out. Not long after, one of their **tenants** reported that the captain's ghost had flown by his bed in the middle of the night. In April 2012, other tenants said that they "felt a really cold chill passing over them—as cold as an iceberg."

A statue of Captain Smith

Captain Smith's boyhood home in Stoke-on-Trent, England

Captain Smith was born in 1850 in the home the Bonners purchased.

Underwater Tomb

The restless spirits of *Titanic*'s victims may walk among the living, but what happened to their bodies? Some of the **corpses** were plucked from the water by rescuers immediately after the disaster. Others drifted in the sea and eventually **decomposed**. Still other victims were pulled to the ocean floor as the ship sank. Then armies of worms, fish, and other sea creatures ate their bodies.

Rescuers look for bodies near an overturned *Titanic* lifeboat.

However, *Titanic* experts like Robert Ballard believe that **preserved** bodies might still be found deep inside the ship. Tom Dettweiler, an explorer who helped discover the sunken ship, agrees. According to him, compartments in the hull could create conditions "known to preserve matter for centuries." Perhaps this can explain the **paranormal** activity reported by vessels cruising above *Titanic*'s watery tomb.

An area of the ship where bodies might still be located

Seventy-three years after it sank, Ballard discovered the *Titanic* on the ocean floor. In 1986, he and other explorers returned with a robot **submarine** to explore the wreck.

13

Phantom Messages

When the *Titanic* made her first—and last—voyage, radios were the newest **technology**. On April 15 at about 12:15 AM as the ship was sinking, Captain Smith ordered radio operator Jack Phillips to send out a **distress** signal. Over and over, Phillips tapped out the plea for help, which was CQD. This code informed other ships to come quickly.

At 11:00 PM on the night of the disaster, the radio operator on a nearby ship warned the *Titanic* of icebergs. Phillips, who was sending messages for the passengers, replied: "Shut up, shut up, I am busy."

Radio operator Jack Phillips

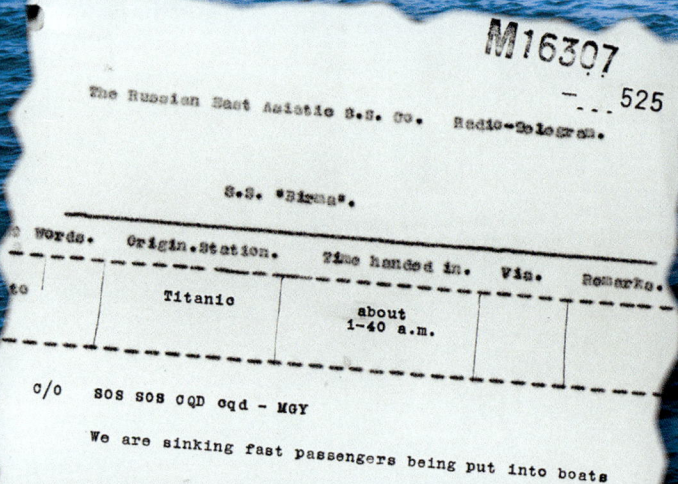

A message from the *Titanic* as it was sinking

Despite the **desperate** calls for help, no ship arrived before the *Titanic* sank. Since that time, ships passing over the site of the disaster have picked up distress signals. Could they be from Phillips, who as the *Titanic* sank, kept signaling until it was too late to board a lifeboat?

What the radio room aboard the *Titanic* might have looked like

Halifax Hauntings

One ship, the *Carpathia*, received Phillips's messages that terrible night. However, it was hours away from the *Titanic*. When the *Carpathia* finally arrived, the *Titanic* had already **plunged** to the ocean floor. The captain scanned the icy ocean water for survivors. They found 705 people.

The *Carpathia*

The *Carpathia* arrived two hours after the *Titanic* sank.

Titanic's survivors aboard the *Carpathia*

As the *Carpathia* carried the survivors to New York City, the *Mackay-Bennett* set sail from Halifax, Canada, with a **gruesome** task. With 100 coffins on board, its job was to bring back the dead. Arriving at the site of the disaster, the crew saw hundreds of frozen corpses floating in the icy water. One survivor, Mary Wilburn, remembered, "The dead came up holding their children in their arms." More than 300 bodies were recovered. Of those, 119 victims were buried at sea, and 209 bodies were transported back to a **morgue** in Halifax. To this day, the building has been a center of paranormal activity.

One of the *Titanic*'s victims aboard a rescue ship

Dining with the Dead

The morgue and funeral home where many of *Titanic*'s victims were housed is now a popular—and haunted—restaurant called The Five Fishermen. Sometimes, spirits appear in a gray mist that rises from the floor. Their faces are often too faded to identify. Other ghosts appear in old-fashioned clothing. Still others are invisible, making their presence known by rattling glasses and throwing objects to the floor.

In the kitchen of The Five Fishermen restaurant in Halifax, water gushes from the faucets when no one is around.

One day while working alone by the salad bar, a waitress felt a hard slap across her face—but no one was around. When she ran to tell another restaurant worker, he immediately saw the red mark on her cheek. Could the unseen hand belong to a long dead *Titanic* passenger whose spirit cannot rest? Might the ghost be angry about being buried so far from home?

A cemetery in Halifax where many *Titanic* victims are buried

Around 150 *Titanic* victims are buried in Halifax. One gravestone belongs to an unknown child. Recently, through scientific testing, the child's body was identified as two-year-old passenger Sidney Leslie Goodwin.

Eternal Vacation

One passenger aboard the *Titanic*, however, may have found his way back home. Millionaire Benjamin Guggenheim traveled in luxury with other first-class passengers. As the ship was sinking, many of them boarded lifeboats, but Guggenheim sat on deck with his assistant. When one of the ship's officers asked what he was doing, he was overheard saying, "We've dressed up in our best and are prepared to go down like gentlemen."

The *Titanic* had many luxuries, including a heated swimming pool and fine restaurants. The most expensive first-class room would have cost around $70,000 in today's money!

An illustration of *Titanic*'s first-class dining room

Guggenheim's body was never recovered from the Atlantic Ocean. However, that doesn't mean he was lost at sea. At a building that was once the Guggenheim family's summer house, a shadowy figure has been seen. It roams around the rooms as lights flicker on and off. Some believe that Guggenheim has returned to his summer home for an **eternal** vacation.

Benjamin Guggenheim

The Guggenheim family's summer house in West Long Branch, New Jersey

Afterlife Reporter

Another famous passenger on the *Titanic* was **journalist** and **spiritualist** W. T. Stead. Before boarding the ship, he met his friend Shaw Desmond in London. Desmond later reported that he felt a sense of "**impending** death." He didn't mention this to Stead, but the feeling was very strong. After the *Titanic* sank, it was reported that Stead had survived. Desmond, however, told Stead's wife, "He is not saved. He is drowned." Unfortunately, his premonition had come true.

W. T. Stead

Even after death, W. T. Stead kept writing. Not long after the deadly accident, he spoke to his daughter through a **medium**. Everything the dead man said was then **transcribed** in a book. It described the sinking *Titanic* in incredible detail—as well as Stead's life after death. This eerie book was published in 1922.

During a séance, people use a medium to try to communicate with the dead.

In 1892, W. T. Stead wrote a book called *From the Old World to the New*. It was about a ship that rescues people after an accident involving an iceberg.

Dead on Display

The restless spirits of other *Titanic* victims have also made themselves known. In 1985, when the *Titanic* was discovered at the bottom of the ocean, so were the belongings of the dead. Tens of thousands of **artifacts** were recovered and then exhibited across the United States. At one exhibition in Atlanta, Georgia, people reported ghostly sightings and voices.

Many artifacts were found preserved in passengers' leather suitcases. The items included pocket watches, binoculars, shoes, and combs.

Personal belongings recovered from the *Titanic*

In 2009, a team of paranormal **investigators** arrived at the exhibit. Not only did the team detect spirits, but they also recorded a ghostly voice. At another *Titanic* exhibit in Las Vegas, one employee took a photograph of a woman in an old-fashioned black dress. He thought she was real, and even spoke to her, but then she vanished before his eyes!

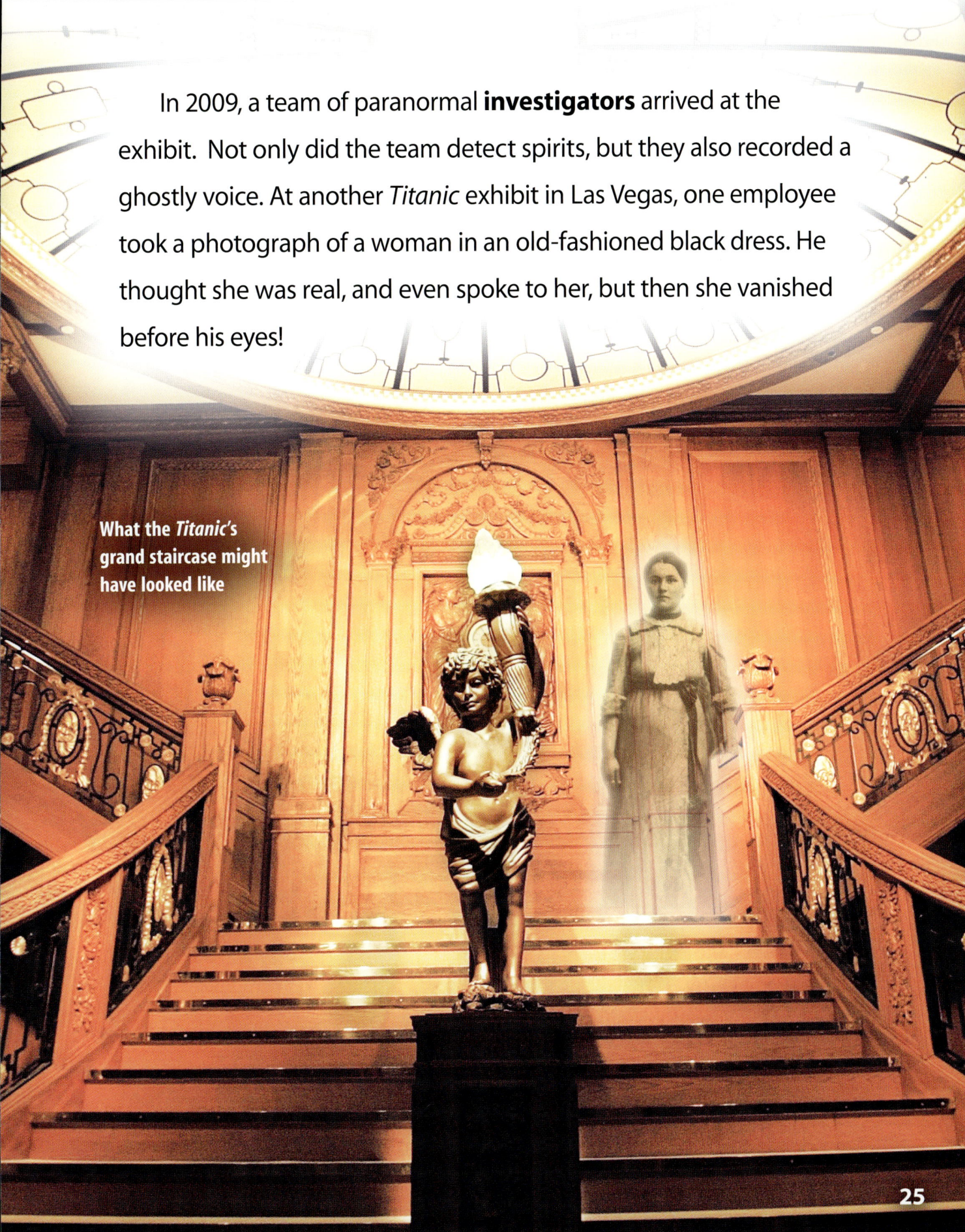

What the *Titanic*'s grand staircase might have looked like

Rest in Peace

When a *Titanic* exhibition toured Wisconsin, one family knew they had to bring their son, Jamey, to see it. Since the age of four, Jamey had been drawing the *Titanic* in amazing detail. In fact, Jamey knew so much about the ship that he sounded like an expert. For example, instead of saying left and right, Jamey said **port** and **starboard**. However, Jamey was also terrified of water and had nightmares of drowning.

The night after visiting the exhibit, Jamey had a horrifying nightmare. His mother remembers hearing her son scream in a man's voice. The boy wailed, "She's going down!" After that night, Jamey talked less and less about the *Titanic*. Today, Jamey, who's now a young man, believes he was **reincarnated** as the *Titanic*'s shipbuilder, Thomas Andrews. Jamey says he finally feels at peace with his past life and the terrible disaster that claimed the great *Titanic* and so many lives.

Thomas Andrews was aboard the *Titanic* when it sank. His body was never found, but he is remembered for helping many people board the lifeboats.

Thomas Andrews

The former home of shipbuilder Thomas Andrews

Titanic: Visions of Doom

Despite the belief that the *Titanic* was unsinkable, many people predicted that the ship would sink. Some of them had spooky dreams or visions of the disaster. Here are a few:

A Bad Fortune

When traveling in Egypt with her family, Alice Fortune met a strange man in her hotel. The man, a fortune teller, warned Alice, "You are in danger every time you travel on the sea, for I see you adrift in an open boat. You will lose everything but your life." A few months later, Alice boarded the *Titanic* in Southampton with her family. She survived the disaster, but her father and brother both died.

It's Going to Sink

As the *Titanic* set sail from Southampton in 1912, people gathered at Jack and Blanche Marshall's house to watch. Blanche, overcome with **dread**, grabbed her husband's arm and cried, "That ship is going to sink before it reaches America!" "Oh, Blanche, it's unsinkable," someone said. "It won't get to America, it will sink, I tell you," she replied loudly. "I can see hundreds of people struggling in the icy water."

Danger!

Violinist Frank Adelman and his wife planned a trip aboard the *Titanic*. Then she had a spooky vision of the ship in danger. To decide whether or not to sail on the *Titanic*, the couple tossed a coin. Mrs. Adelman won. They wouldn't be sailing on the ship—or risking their lives.

Glossary

artifacts (ART-uh-fakts) objects of historical interest that were made by people

coma (KOH-muh) a state in which a person is unconscious and cannot wake up

corpses (KORPS-iz) dead bodies

dead ringer (DED RING-ur) a person or thing that looks exactly like someone or something else

decomposed (dee-kuhm-POHZD) rotted or decayed

desperate (DESS-pur-it) feeling hopeless

distress (diss-TRESS) needing help

doom (DOOM) ruin or death

dread (DRED) fear

eternal (i-TUR-nuhl) endless

feverish (FEE-vur-ish) experiencing a rise in body temperature

foresee (fawr-SEE) to know in advance

gruesome (GROO-suhm) horrible; causing horror or disgust

hull (HUHL) the frame or body of a ship

impending (im-PEND-ing) when something is about to happen

investigators (in-VEST-uh-gay-torz) people who study events or collect information about things

journalist (JUR-nhl-ist) a person who writes for newspapers or magazines

medium (MEE-dee-uhm) a person claiming to be in contact with the spirits of the dead

morgue (MORG) a place where dead bodies are kept before being buried

ocean liner (OH-shun LIE-nuhr) a passenger ship that transports people across the ocean

orphan (OR-fuhn) a child whose parents are dead

paranormal (pa-ruh-NOR-muhl) supernatural; not able to be explained by science

plunged (PLUNJD) fell quickly

port (PORT) the left side of a ship

premonition (preh-mun-ISH-uhn) a strong feeling that something is about to happen

preserved (pri-ZURVD) protected or kept safe from injury

reincarnated (ree-in-KAHR-neyt-uhd) reborn in another body

spiritualist (SPIR-i-choo-uhl-ist) a person who believes in the world of ghosts and spirits

starboard (STAR-burd) the right side of a ship

submarine (SUHB-muh-reen) a ship that can travel underwater

technology (tek-NOL-uh-jee) the science of making useful things

tenants (TEN-uhnts) people who rent a property from someone else

transcribed (tran-SKRYBD) put into written form

vanished (VAN-ishd) disappeared from sight

Bibliography

Broad, William J. "Experts Split on Possibility of Remains at *Titanic* Site." *The New York Times* (April 14, 2012).

Holman, Hannah. *Titanic Voices: 63 Survivors Tell Their Extraordinary Stories*. Gloucestershire, England: Amberley (2011).

Wilson, Andrew. *Shadow of the Titanic: The Extraordinary Stories of Those Who Survived*. New York: Simon & Schuster (2011).

Read More

Blake, Kevin. *Creating Titanic: The Ship of Dreams (Titanica)*. New York: Bearport (2018).

Blake, Kevin. *Titanic's Fatal Voyage (Titanica)*. New York: Bearport (2018).

Lawson, Julie. *Ghosts of the Titanic*. New York: Holiday House (2012).

Learn More Online

To learn more about the haunted *Titanic*, visit
www.bearportpublishing.com/Titanica

Dishes from the *Titanic*

Index

Andrews, Thomas 27
artifacts 24
Atlantic Ocean 4, 7, 17, 21

Ballard, Robert 13

Carpathia 16–17
corpses 12, 17

Desmond, Shaw 22
Dettweiler, Tom 13

ghosts 8–9, 10-11, 12, 18–19, 21, 24–25
Guggenheim, Benjamin 20–21

Halifax 17, 18–19
Hartley, Wallace 5, 8–9
hull 5, 13

iceberg 4–5, 7, 8, 11, 14, 23

journalist 22

lifeboats 7, 12, 15, 20, 27

Mackay-Bennett 17
medium 23
morgue 17, 18

paranormal activity 13, 17, 18–19, 20–21, 23, 24–25
Phillips, Jack 14–15
premonition 8, 22

radio signals 14–15
reincarnation 27
Robertson, Morgan 6–7

Sayre, Jessie 4–5, 6, 8
Smith, Captain Edward John 10–11, 14
Smith, Eleanor 10
Stead, W. T. 22–23
submarine 13

Titan 6–7

Wilburn, Mary 17

About the Author

E. Merwin writes stories, books, and poems for kids and adults. Since she began writing about ghosts and haunted places, she has been sleeping with the lights on.

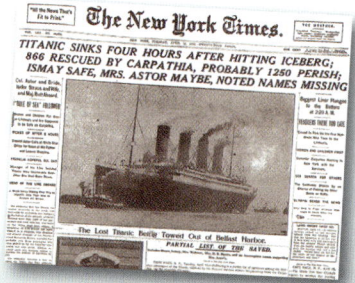